23 £2-50

Embroidery on Paper:
Alphabet and Festive Motifs

Joke and Adriaan de Vette

D1099081

Search Press

Contents

I would like to thank the following for their help in the realisation of this book:
my husband, Adriaan, for making up templates and text;
Sjaak van Went for making up and elaborating the templates;
Ms J. Koops for help with the embroidery;
Sandra Broekhuizen for her organisation and some of the design work.

Thanks to the following for making materials available:
Kars – paper for the letter cards and beads;
Avec – paper;
Romak – cards and 3D prints;
Nielsen – 3D prints;
DMC – mixed stranded thread.

First published in Great Britain 2009 by Search Press Limited, Wellwood, North Farm Road, Tunbridge Wells, Kent TN2 3DR

Copyright © 2008 Tirion Uitgevers BV
This book is published by Cantecleer
Cantecleer is an imprint of Tirion Publishers BV

English translation by Cicero Translations
English edition edited and typeset by GreenGate Publishing Services, Tonbridge

All rights reserved. No part of this book, text, photographs or illustrations may be reproduced or transmitted in any form or by any means by print, photoprint, microfilm, microfiche, photocopier, internet or in any way known or as yet unknown, or stored in a retrieval system, without written permission obtained beforehand from Search Press.

ISBN: 978-1-84448-461-4

Suppliers
If you have any difficulty in obtaining any of the materials and equipment mentioned in this book, please visit the Search Press website for details of other suppliers:
www.searchpress.com

Although every attempt has been made to ensure that all the materials and equipment used in this book are currently available, the Publishers cannot guarantee that this will always be the case. If you have difficulty in obtaining any of the items mentioned, then suitable alternatives should be used instead.

Design: ZieZo Design, Maarssen
Photography: Hennie Raaijmakers, St. Michielsgestel
Templates: Sjaak van Went, Leiden
Dutch edition edited by Loes Brouwer

Foreword

After a year's silence, I am now happy to be able to present my new book, *Embroidery on Paper: Alphabet and Festive Motifs*. The book is almost too full, containing twenty festive cards in addition to the twenty-six letters of the alphabet. Most of these cards were thought up, drawn and developed into embroidery templates by my husband, Adriaan. This was an extremely time-consuming job but now everything is finished. The cards give this book an extra dimension. The letters are elegantly formed, making them very suitable for birthdays and anniversaries. They can be embroidered on to relatively small cards so that, for example, combinations of two letters on one card can easily be achieved. All the templates are shown actual size.

Once again, I wish you much pleasure in your embroidery.

Materials required

- Piercing mat, for instance two layers of craft foam
- Fine piercing tool (e.g. Pergamano single-point piercing tool)
- Thin embroidery needles
- (Sewing machine) embroidery threads (e.g. Sulky, Madeira and Gütermann)
- Cards or paper, 170–250g (6–8¾oz)
- White paper inserts, 120g (4¼oz)
- Copies of pricking templates
- 3D designs, Mireille and Romak
- Adhesive tape
- Paperclips
- 3D kit
- Water-free glue (e.g. photo adhesive or UHU magic stick)
- 0.3mm (⅛in) propelling pencil or sharp HB pencil
- Eraser
- Optional: cutting mat, craft knife and ruler
- Optional: small adhesive gemstones in various colours

General instructions

Template

Use a photocopier to copy the templates from the book. Cut out the template and attach it firmly to the card with paperclips. You can also use removable tape to attach the template. This is much more satisfactory than conventional plastic adhesive tape. A frame has been drawn around each template to help you place the template correctly on the card. Most of the frames are smaller than the card. If you are using paperclips, cut out the template a little more generously, for example as wide as the card, otherwise you will not be able to attach the template properly to the card.

Pricking out the design

Place the card on which the design is to be pricked out, together with the template, on a piercing mat. Use a fine piercing tool for pricking out and hold it as upright as possible. Try to prick out all the holes as accurately as possible because clean pricking makes for beautiful work. Do not make the holes too big because when you are embroidering you repeatedly have to turn the card over to see where to put the needle. If the holes are too big, the needle will fall out of the card. A fairly thin piercing mat (two layers of craft foam, about 4mm; ¼in thick) works very well.

Embroidery

The cards in this book were embroidered with Sulky threads, unless otherwise stated. The colours and embroidery stitches used are given for each card.

Finishing touches

Once the embroidery work is completed, the pricked-out holes may be annoyingly visible. To solve this problem, use a smooth convex object to rub the holes closed on the back of the card after embroidering. A clean teaspoon works well.

Tape a white insert over the back of the embroidery. You could also stick the embroidered card on to another card. If photo glue oozes under the edge, you can rub it off with your finger or a cloth. You can rub off dried glue with your finger or the tip of an eraser.

N.B. Limit skin contact with wet glue: glue may cause a skin reaction.

Embroidery stitches

The description of the embroidery stitches may be different from what you are used to. I want to give you an understanding of the various stitches so that in future you will be able to embroider easily without charts. Many stitches with different names are similar to one another; only the shape is different because the pricked-out holes form a different pattern. The basic stitch is drawn in bold lines in the diagrams showing the embroidery stitches. Repetitions are drawn in fine lines.

Long stitch

Long stitch is simply a thread between two pricked-out holes (not illustrated).

Back stitch

Back stitch is only used to embroider very thin lines or small curves, such as a small eye. Push the needle through the first hole in the line from back to front, from front to back through the second hole, back to front through the third, and so on. Stitch first in one direction and then in the other, as in the diagram, in order to obtain a solid line.

Back stitch

Stem stitch

Stem stitch is used for slightly larger details and slightly thicker lines. Push the needle through the first hole in the line from back to front. Move two holes forwards on the front of the card and one hole backwards on the reverse. This is the basis of stem stitch. Repeat this basic stitch.

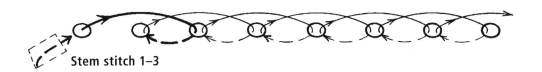

Stem stitch 1–3

Long stem stitch (simple)

Long stem stitch produces a rope-like embroidered line. Long stem stitch can be worked in either of two ways. The simple method has the same shape as normal stem stitch but you leave a larger distance when you move forwards and backwards. For example, move forwards four holes on the front (1–5) and three holes backwards on the reverse, as in the diagram. The stitch can also be made longer or shorter.

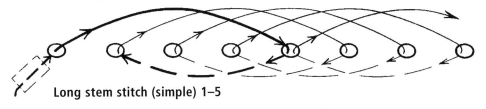

Long stem stitch (simple) 1–5

Thin ends

The beginning and end of a line of long stem stitch are often a bit thin. Fill them out with a few shorter stitches. This applies to both versions of long stem stitch.

Shortening and lengthening long stem stitch

If you are approaching a short curve or if you want a thinner line, switch to a shorter stitch. Once you have passed the curve or if you want a thicker line, switch to a longer stitch. This works for both versions of long stem stitch.

TIP: Do not think about it too much, just follow your instincts.

Long stem stitch (normal)

This method provides the same rope-like line as the simple version but very little thread is left on the reverse of the card. This means that the reverse of the card will be tidier and you will be able to embroider more easily.

As you can see from the diagram, you move backwards and forwards on the front of the card using stitches of the same length each time. On the reverse of the card, you move forwards one hole each time. Make the basic stitch shown in bold lines and repeat this. You can also choose to make the stitch shorter or longer than the one shown in the diagram. The small stitches on the reverse do not change.

These small stitches on the reverse help you to keep the length of the stitches constant. With a stitch length of 1–5, 1–7, 1–9, etc., the small stitches on the reverse will form a solid line (this does not apply to the first couple of stitches).

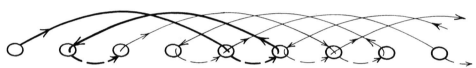

Long stem stitch (normal) 1–5

Circle stitch

Circle stitch is similar to long stem stitch (normal) but easier to make because you can see what you are doing so well.

Make the basic stitch shown in bold print (see diagram A). Repeat the basic stitch until the circle is complete (see diagrams B and C). You will then have two threads in each hole. You can also make a circle stitch using shorter or longer stitches.

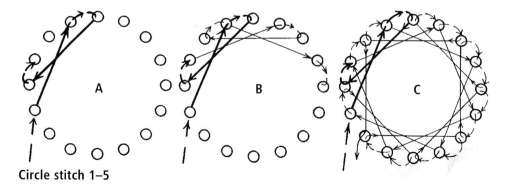

Circle stitch 1–5

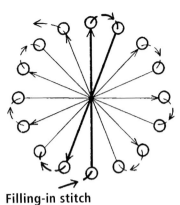

Filling-in stitch

Filling-in stitch is a special form of circle stitch. It is used to completely fill in circles and stars etc. The first stitch runs on the front, through the middle to the opposite side of the shape. There must be an even number of holes to the left and right of the first stitch otherwise it will not work out.

Work the basic stitch shown in bold print and repeat it until the shape is filled in. All the small stitches on the reverse run in the same direction. To remind you, draw an arrow on the reverse before you start embroidering.

Filling-in stitch

Fan stitch

Fan stitch is used to fill in flower petals and similar shapes. The central hole needs to be made considerably larger than the other pricked-out holes.

Stitch through the central hole from back to front. Pass the needle to the reverse at the edge of the shape and back through the central hole to the front. This is the basis of fan stitch. Repeat the stitch until the shape has been filled in.

Try to avoid crossed threads as follows: with each thread that you embroider from the centre to the edge, skip a few holes along the edge (see diagram A). When you have reached the end of the shape, embroider another thread into each gap (see diagram B). After, say, four rounds of the shape it will be entirely filled in (see diagram C).

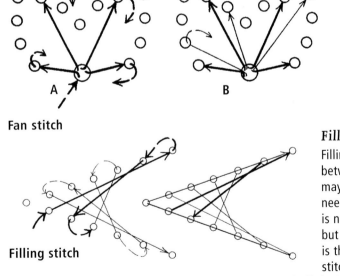

Fan stitch

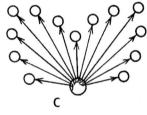

Filling stitch

Filling stitch fills the space between two lines. The lines may meet at one end but they need not do so. Stitch length is not always the same here but the method of embroidery is the same as for long stem stitch (normal) and circle stitch.

Filling stitch

Do not embroider the lines over the rows of holes until all the intersecting lines have been embroidered.

Floral letters A to F

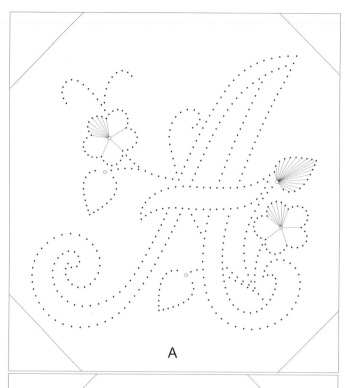

A

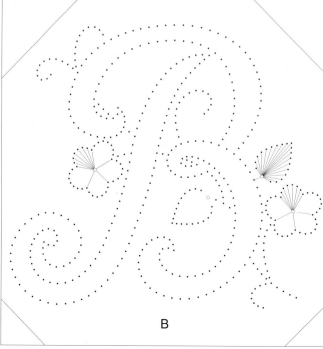

B

The design of the letters is simple yet elegant. The floral sprig gives the letter a celebratory air. Each letter can be embroidered on a rectangular card (about 13.5 × 9.5cm; 5¼ × 3¾in), in a diamond shape (about 10.5 × 10.5cm; 4¼ × 4¼in) or in a circle (about 10.5cm; 4¼in). Examples of each can be seen in the various chapters of this book. Two embroidered cards can also be glued to a larger card. The combination of two letters is often useful for weddings and anniversaries. If you want to fill a standard-sized card with one letter, it is a good idea to enlarge this letter by about 25 per cent.

The letters are embroidered on particularly pretty paper (cArt-us card, spiders web crème, A4 240g/8½oz, from Kars, item number 651696/0924). The paper makes the card even more suitable for celebratory occasions.

The templates for the letters are provided in alphabetical order in the four letter chapters of the book. Letters Y and Z can be found on page 48.

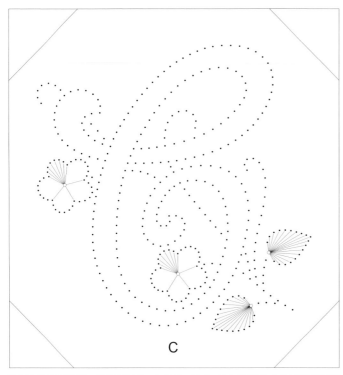

C

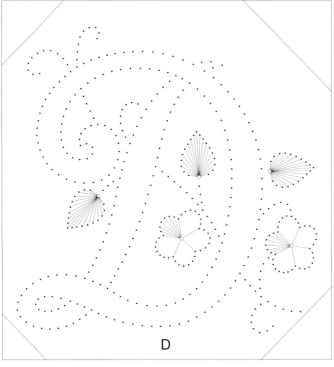

D

Embroider the letter using Sulky gold 7007 thread and long stem stitch. The stitch length most frequently used is 1–5 (from hole 1 to hole 5 on the front of the card). If you want to make the long lines extra thick, you should choose a stitch length of 1–6 or 1–7. To keep the line fluid in the short curves, switch to a stitch length of 1–4 or 1–3. Use your own judgement to decide when to switch to a larger or smaller stitch length. If part of a line is too thin, go over it with a couple of extra stitches.

The stem of the sprig of flowers is embroidered with long stem stitch. Use fan stitch for the flowers and leaves. The thread used is DMC stranded thread.

You can find diagrams and descriptions of all the embroidery stitches used in the general instructions at the start of this book (page 4).

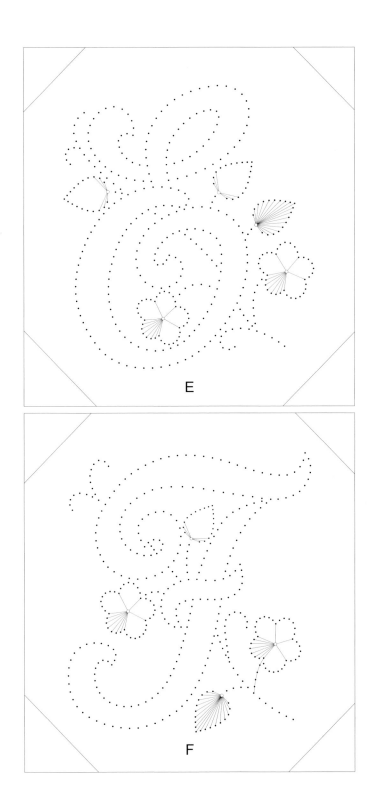

E

F

Christmas night

When thinking of Christmas night, it is not unusual to combine various figures with the moon. The moon is a good frame for the subjects. Embroider on to cards that are a little larger than the templates.

Clear diagrams and descriptions of the embroidery stitches used and other useful information can be found in the general instructions at the start of this book (page 4).

The moon

Do not embroider the moon until all the other components have been embroidered. This is the only way that you will be able to see clearly which parts of the moon need to go behind tree branches, and so on. Use Sulky gold 7007 and long stem stitch 1–5 to embroider the moon. Let the embroidery thin out at the pointed ends of the moon. Embroider those parts of the moon between the branches with a few extra stitches to give a strong line.

Embroidering details

The shape of the details – particularly faces – is important. Use back stitch first to obtain a good shape. Then embroider over this with stem stitch 1–3 to make the lines a bit thicker.

2A

Stop the stem stitch when you reach a corner; push the needle through to the reverse of the card, run it beneath the other embroidery and bring it back to the front through the same hole. Start on the next line.

Girl in moon

The threads used are Sulky olive green 7056 for the trees, lavender 7012 for the skin colour, red 7013 for the dress, black 7051 for the shoes, and light copper 7011 for the lantern. Yellowish rayon thread was used for the hair and the base line. Embroider the figure using stem stitch for the shoes, for example, and long stem stitch 1–4 and 1–5 for the longer lines. Long stitch and filling-in stitch are used in the lantern. See also 'Embroidering details' on page 12.

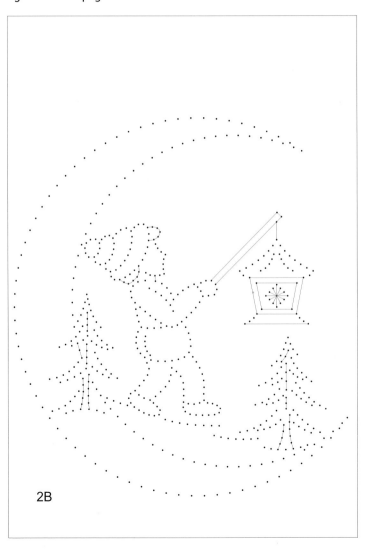

2B

Boy in moon

The threads used are Sulky lavender 7012 for the face and hand, together with green 7018, blue 7016, red 7013 and light copper 7011. Embroider the figure with stem stitch and long stem stitch 1–4. Long stitch and filling-in stitch are used in the lantern. See also 'Embroidering details' above.

Nativity scene in moon

Embroider the figures in clear, cheerful colours to create an evocative picture. The colours used here are lavender 7012 for the skin, light copper 7011 for the hair, clothing and manger, together with black/silver 7023 and deep blue 7016 for the clothing. The base lines are dark copper 7010.

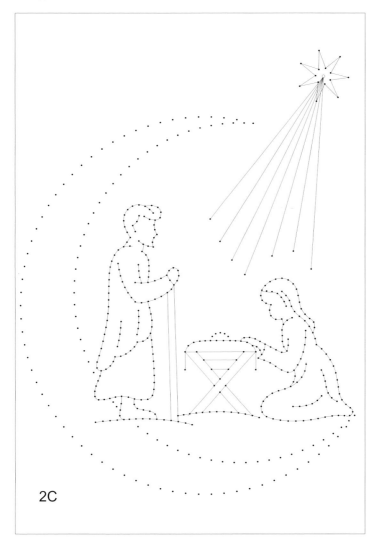

2C

Floral letters G to J

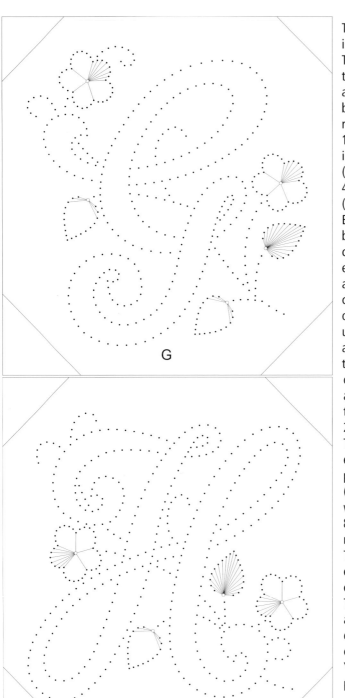

G

H

The design of the letters is simple yet elegant. The floral sprig gives the letter a celebratory air. Each letter can be embroidered on a rectangular card (about 13.5 × 9.5cm; 5¼ × 3¾in), in a diamond shape (about 10.5 × 10.5cm; 4¼ × 4¼in) or in a circle (about 10.5cm; 4¼in). Examples of each can be seen in the various chapters of this book. Two embroidered cards can also be glued to a larger card. The combination of two letters is often useful for weddings and anniversaries. If you want to fill a standard-sized card with one letter, it is a good idea to enlarge this letter by about 25 per cent.

The letters are embroidered on particularly pretty paper (cArt-us card, spiders web crème, A4 240g; 8½oz, from Kars, item number 651696/0924). The paper makes the card even more suitable for celebratory occasions. The templates for the letters are provided in alphabetical order in the four letter chapters of the book. Letters Y and Z can be found on page 48.

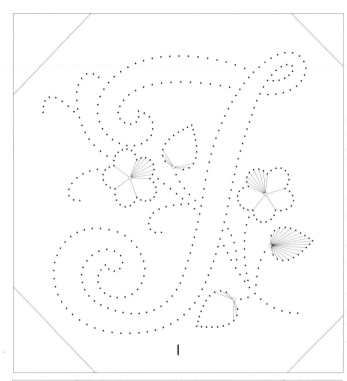

I

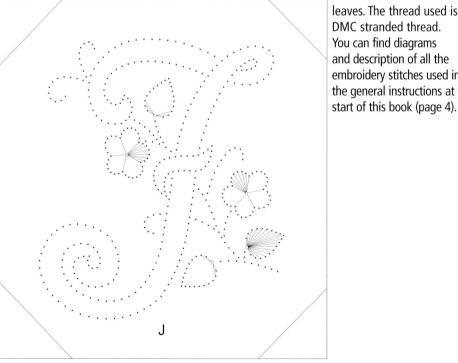

J

Embroider the letter using Sulky gold 7007 thread and long stem stitch. The stitch length most frequently used is 1–5 (from hole 1 to hole 5 on the front of the card). If you want to make the long lines extra thick, you should choose a stitch length of 1–6 or 1–7. To keep the line fluid in the short curves, switch to a stitch length of 1–4 or 1–3. Use your own judgement to decide when to switch to a larger or smaller stitch length. If part of a line is too thin, go over it with a couple of extra stitches. The stem of the sprig of flowers is embroidered with long stem stitch. Use fan stitch for the flowers and leaves. The thread used is DMC stranded thread. You can find diagrams and description of all the embroidery stitches used in the general instructions at the start of this book (page 4).

Candlestick

Use the template to prick out the candlestick design on the card. First embroider the candle flame using fan stitch. Make the bottommost hole of the flame, the central hole, larger than the others. From this hole, first embroider towards the side edges and then move gradually towards the top. Embroider each candle as shown in the diagram alongside. First work the stitches as shown in A. Then embroider the first cross stitch (see B). Embroider the second and third cross stitches (see C and D). Carry on in this way until the whole candle is filled in. Embroider the straight stitches of the base two or three times to make the lines a bit thicker. Embroider the rest using long stem stitch.

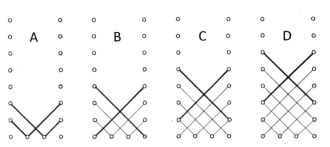

Christmas stars

There are a number of motifs available to us when we want to decorate our home for Christmas: red and white Christmas bells, green branches, candles, baubles and stars. In the cards in this chapter, a star is used as a frame for three other Christmas decorations. Tips, diagrams and descriptions of the embroidery stitches can be found at the start of this book.

The star

The star can be embroidered easily and fairly quickly. See the diagram for filling stitch on page 7. First embroider the cross-threads in every point of the star and then the lines that cover the holes for every point. The thread is Sulky gold 7007. Use circle stitch with a stitch length of 1–7 (from hole 1 to hole 7) for the large circle. All the cards are 13cm (5in) square.

Candles in star

First embroider the side edges of the candles. Look on the template to see which of the pricked-out holes are used for these. Embroider each line three times to make the line thicker. Use stem stitch for the upper edge of the candles and long stem stitch 1–4 for the flames.

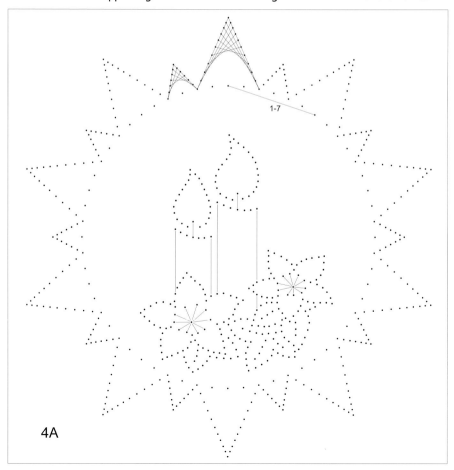

4A

Start embroidering at the top of the flame. Leave the topmost point thin. The flame is open at the bottom, as in a real candle flame.

Embroider flowers and greenery with long stem stitch 1–4 and use fan stitch for the stamens. Embroider the stamens twice.

The threads used are Sulky gold 7007 and green 7015. Red stranded thread is used for the flowers.

Pine cones in star

Embroider the branch using long stem stitch 1–5 and 7011 light copper thread. Look at the template to see how to embroider the pine needles.

The topmost scales of the pine cones are green, as are the needles. It may be useful to draw the scales of the pine cones lightly on to the card with a pencil. Refer to the template for this. The lines of the scales do not touch one another.

If you want to fill out the lines prettily, first work the scales in back stitch and then embroider over this with stem stitch. Use long stem stitch for the slightly longer lines. For each scale, work the stem stitch and long stem stitch from the top to the lowest point; stop there and embroider the other side from top to bottom again.

The threads used are Sulky olive green 7056 and light copper 7011.

4B

Christmas bells in star

First embroider the pine twigs and the zigzag border in the bells as drawn on the template. Embroider the zigzag border as shown in the diagram alongside. Embroider the lines above

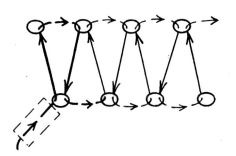

and below the zigzag border using back stitch. Make the back stitches a little larger by skipping a hole each time. Use stem stitch for the upper decorative border on the bells and for the clapper. Work the outer line of the bells using long stem stitch 1–4 or 1–5. Use long stem stitch 1–5 for the golden ribbons.
The threads used are Sulky gold 7007, red 7013 and green 7015.

1-7

4C

Christmas with 3D birds

We see birds all year round, particularly in our home surroundings where they have become completely used to people. A piece of bread or some peanuts are usually enough to attract them. These popular little creatures are often depicted on Christmas cards and we have three old favourites in this chapter. They are all to be found on the step-by-step sheet from Mireille X176 (Nielsen, Rotterdam). The robin is still the most timid, but the blue tit with its pale blue cap and the sparrow are almost impertinent.

Because 3D designs for Christmas generally involve the same colours, you can easily use other 3D designs in these templates. The space in the templates for use with 3D designs varies so that different designs will fit in.

The cards used are by Romak, 12.5 × 12.5cm (5 × 5in).

Clear diagrams and descriptions of the embroidery stitches used and other useful information can be found in the general instructions at the start of this book (page 4).

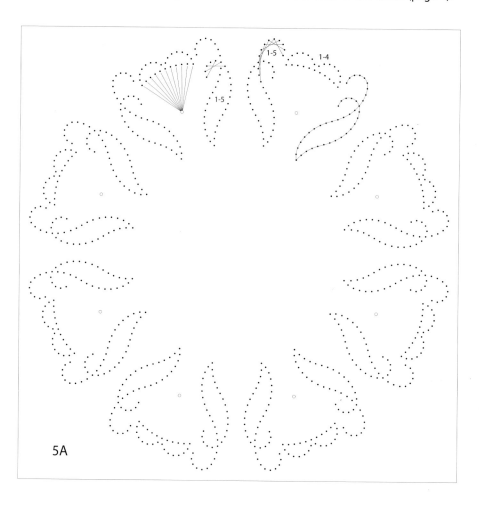

5A

Robin redbreast

Prick out the design from the template 5A on to the card. Make the central hole for the red fans slightly larger than the other pricked-out holes. Embroider the fans in fan stitch using the instructions on page 7. Use long stem stitch 1–4 for the green arches above each fan. Work the golden curlicues in long stem stitch 1–5.
The threads are Sulky gold 7007, red 7013 and green 7015.

Blue tit in star garland

Prick out the design from template 5B on to the card. Embroider the stars as shown in the template. The long threads linking the stars provide some filling behind the 3D embellishment. You could also stretch these threads across in other ways. The threads used are Sulky red 7013 and green 7015.

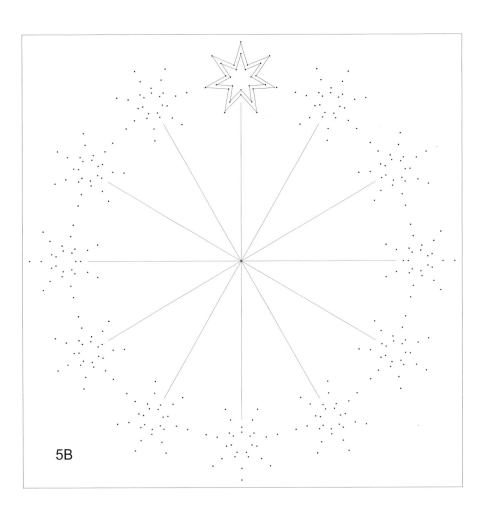

5B

Sparrow

Prick out the design from template 5C on to the card.

Look at the instructions on the template to see how to embroider the red chalices. Proceed as follows to minimise the risk of undesired crossing of the threads: first embroider one half of the chalice from 1 to A, go back on the reverse and embroider from 2 to B and so on up to a thread from 7 to G. Embroider the other half of the chalice in the same way. Finally embroider the thread from 7 to G that covers the holes.

For the other figures, first embroider the loop shape, starting with the wider end and using stem stitch 1–5. Work the curved fronds with a slightly shorter stitch 1–4. The threads are Sulky gold 7007 and red 7013.

5C

Borders with 3D designs

You will find diagrams and descriptions of all the embroidery stitches at the start of this book. Other festive embellishments will also fit into the embroidery templates in this chapter. Because red and green are usually the main colours of these prints, the cards can always be embroidered with red, green and gold. All the cards are 12.5 × 12.5cm (5 × 5in).

Bell-ringer and girl on Christmas bauble

The prints are Ritva's Fairies (Romak PO-300-05). The two pieces of embroidery are variations of the same template. The template for the bell-ringer leaves space for a wide design; the other template allows greater height. The colours of the threads are in keeping with many Christmas embellishments, but if you use different colours of thread, you can use the templates with any designs. The pricked-out template will become clearer once you have embroidered the red lines. Work these red lines as two smooth, wavy lines that intersect repeatedly. Embroider the first line from top to bottom, flowing to the left, then to the right, and so on. Use long stem stitch 1–5 and Sulky red 7013. Do the same for the second red line.

Embroider the green angled shapes using filling stitch and green thread 7018. Threads covering the holes are always worked last. Finally, embroider the small shapes between the red lines using filling-in stitch, and the little fans using fan stitch with gold thread 7007.

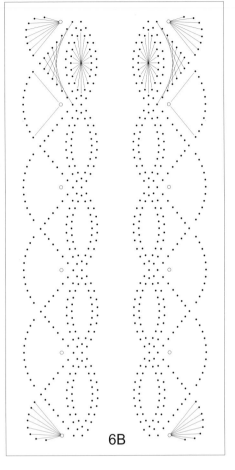

6B

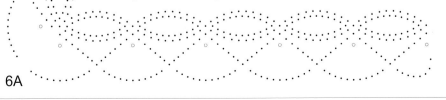

6A

Deer with squirrels

Using template 6C, prick out one half on to the left side of the embroidery card and the other half on to the right.
Embroider the green fans using fan stitch and the red angled shapes using filling stitch. The threads are olive green 7056 and red 7013. Work the curlicues with mixed red/green/gold 7027 using long stem stitch. Use a stitch length of 1–7 for the large curlicue and 1–5 for the small one. The embellishment is from Mireille X191 (Nielsen, Rotterdam).

Deer with rabbits

Using template 6D, prick out one half on to the left side of the embroidery card and the other half on to the right. Look at the instructions on the pricking template to see how to embroider the red chalices. Proceed as follows to minimise the risk of undesired crossing of the threads: first embroider one half of the chalice from 1 to A, go back on the reverse and then embroider from 2 to B and so on up to a thread from 6 to F. Embroider the other half of the chalice in the same way. Finally embroider the thread from 6 to F that covers the holes. For the other figures, first embroider the loop shape starting with the wider end, and then the curved fronds. Use long stem stitch 1–5. The threads are mixed red/green/gold 7027 and the embellishment is from Mireille X191 (Nielsen, Rotterdam).

6C

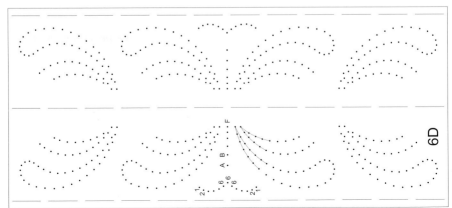

6D

Floral letters K to R

K

L

The design of the letters is simple yet elegant. The floral sprig gives the letter a celebratory air. Each letter can be embroidered on a rectangular card (about 13.5 × 9.5cm; 5¼ × 3¾in), in a diamond shape (about 10.5 × 10.5cm; 4¼ × 4¼in) or in a circle (about 10.5cm; 4¼in). Examples of each can be seen in the various chapters of this book. Two embroidered cards can also be glued to a larger card. The combination of two letters is often useful for weddings and anniversaries. If you want to fill a standard-sized card with one letter, it is a good idea to enlarge this letter by about 25 per cent.

The letters are embroidered on particularly pretty paper (cArt-us card, spiders web crème, A4 240g; 8½oz, from Kars, item number 651696/0924). The paper makes the card even more suitable for celebratory occasions. The templates for the letters are provided in alphabetical order in the four letter chapters of the book. Letters Y and Z can be found on page 48.

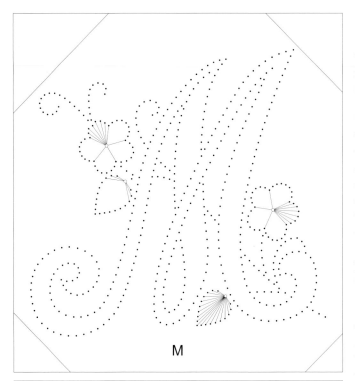

M

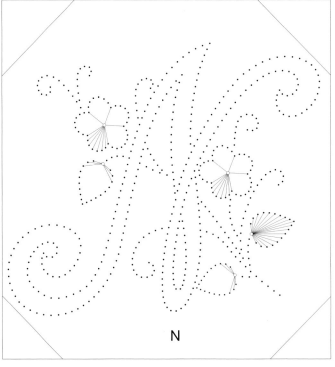

N

Embroider the letter using Sulky gold 7007 thread and long stem stitch. The stitch length most frequently used is 1–5 (from hole 1 to hole 5 on the front of the card). If you want to make the long lines extra thick, you should choose a stitch length of 1–6 or 1–7. To keep the line fluid in the short curves, switch to a stitch length of 1–4 or 1–3. Use your own judgement to decide when to switch to a larger or smaller stitch length. If part of a line is too thin, go over it with a couple of extra stitches. The stem of the sprig of flowers is embroidered with long stem stitch. Use fan stitch for the flowers and leaves. The thread used is DMC stranded thread.

You can find diagrams and descriptions of all the embroidery stitches used in the general instructions at the start of this book (page 4).

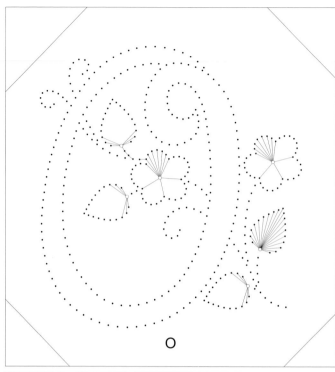

O

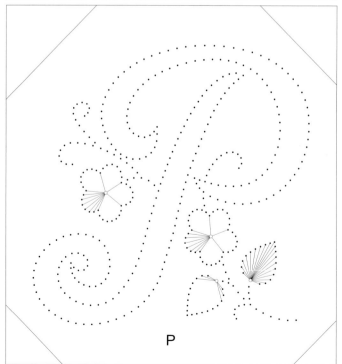

P

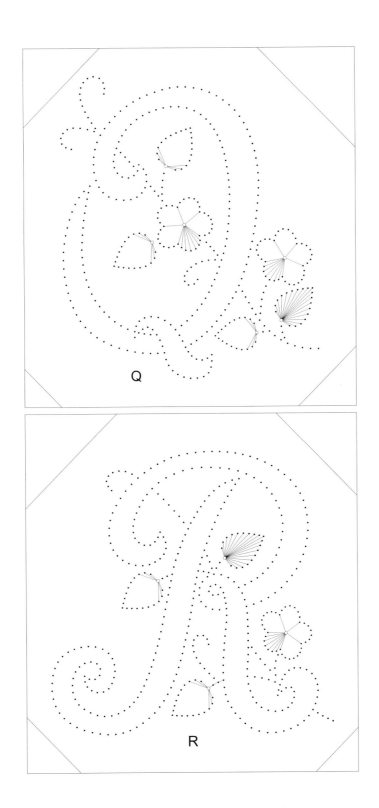

Q

R

Oh Christmas tree!

Every Christmas, many of us will buy a Christmas tree and decorate it as beautifully as possible. The Christmas tree is also a rewarding subject for embroidery. The tree itself is simple and fairly quick to embroider. Inside the tree, you can work one of three subjects or mount a 3D embellishment.
The threads used are Sulky olive green 7056, gold 7007, dark copper 7010 for the manger, lavender 7012 for skin colour, light copper 7011 for hair and clothing and also purple 7050 and deep blue 7016. The cards are 13 × 13cm (5 × 5in) in size.

Embroidering the tree

Use long stem stitch 1-7 for most of the branches and a stitch length of 1-5 for short, curved branches. Leave the thin ends of the stem stitch as they are as this will highlight the shape of the branches. Work a few stitches over one another at your own discretion for the small branches on the underside. The star can be embroidered in various ways, as described for the individual cards.

8A

Tree with flower arrangement

The effect of this template is even better on a paler colour card. Prick out the design from template 8A on to the card. You will see small arrows in the lines for the candles. Prick a very small hole at the site of the arrows. No thread will go through this hole; it is just a guide. Work each thread from the top to the bottom in a straight line over the small hole. Do this three times so as to make them a bit thicker. Embroider the rest of the candles using long stem stitch, about 1–4. Work the flowers with long stem stitch, about 1–6. Vary the stitch length as you see fit.

Tree with nativity scene

The shape of the details – particularly faces – is extremely important. See the paragraph on 'Embroidering details' on pages 12 and 14. Embroider the rest of the people with (long) stem stitch 1–3, 1–4 and 1–5. Keep the folds in the clothing very thin. Stop at each corner and start afresh. Use cheerful colours (see page 36).

8B

Tree with lights

First embroider all the candles, then the tree and finally the star and its rays. This will mean that the green will go over the base of each candle. For the candles, start with the diagonal lines and then work the outer edges each time.

Use fan stitch for the flames. Make the central hole slightly larger than the others. Push the needle from the reverse to the front through the central hole, pull the thread in the required direction and push the needle back to the reverse through one of the holes at the edge. Repeat this procedure. Start with the holes at the bottom left and right edges and end in the middle at the top.

8C

Floral letters S to Z

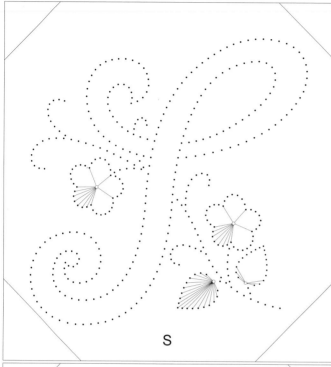

S

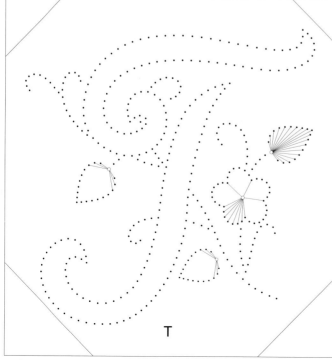

T

The design of the letters is simple yet elegant. The floral sprig gives the letter a celebratory air. Each letter can be embroidered on a rectangular card (about 13.5 × 9.5cm; 5¼ × 3¾in), in a diamond shape (about 10.5 × 10.5cm; 4¼ × 4¼in) or in a circle (about 10.5cm; 4¼in). Examples of each can be seen in the various chapters of this book. Two embroidered cards can also be glued to a larger card. The combination of two letters is often useful for weddings and anniversaries. If you want to fill a standard-sized card with one letter, it is a good idea to enlarge this letter by about 25 per cent.

The letters are embroidered on particularly pretty paper (cArt-us card, spiders web crème, A4 240g; 8½oz, from Kars, item number 651696/0924). The paper makes the card even more suitable for celebratory occasions. The templates for the letters are provided in alphabetical order in the four letter chapters of the book. Letters Y and Z can be found on page 48.

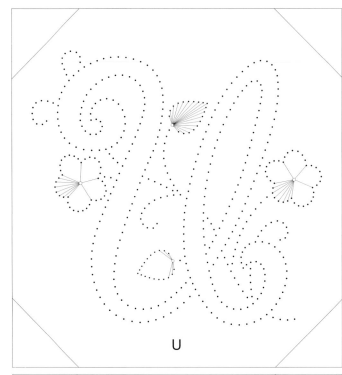

U

Embroider the letter using Sulky gold 7007 thread and long stem stitch. The stitch length most frequently used is 1–5 (from hole 1 to hole 5 on the front of the card). If you want to make the long lines extra thick, you should choose a stitch length of 1–6 or 1–7. To keep the line fluid in the short curves, switch to a stitch length of 1–4 or 1–3. Use your own judgement to decide when to switch to a larger or smaller stitch length. If part of a line is too thin, go over it with a couple of extra stitches. The stem of the sprig of flowers is embroidered with long stem stitch. Use fan stitch for the flowers and leaves. The thread used is DMC stranded thread. You can find diagrams and descriptions of all the embroidery stitches used in the general instructions at the start of this book (page 4).

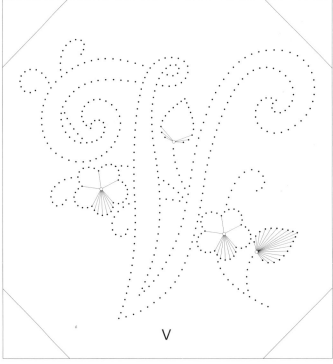

V

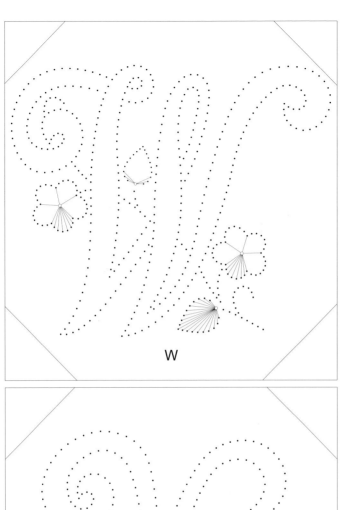

W

X

Christmas with beads

This last chapter contains three cards that have been based, with a little imagination, on conventional Christmas decorations. Beads, embossing and cutwork make the cards extra cheerful. You could also make the corners of the cards more simple or embroider the main motif on to a smaller card. Template 10A shows embroidery in the corners. In the general instructions at the start of this book, you will find clear diagrams and descriptions of the embroidery stitches used and other useful instructions. The cards used are 12.5 × 12.5cm (5 × 5in) in size.

The corners

The corners of the examples illustrated are embossed, cut and embroidered using a small stencil from Joycraft, no. 6001/0053. If you want to make the cards in the same way, draw pencil lines on the front of the card about 3mm (⅛in) in from the edges of the card. Place the stencil in one corner, aligned against the pencil lines. Tape the stencil firmly in place.

10A

Use a pencil to outline the openings you want to cut out; emboss the other openings and prick out the holes for the embroidery. You will find instructions for the embroidery on the stencil. It is easier to cut along a pencil line than along an embossed line and the effect is prettier. After you have finished cutting, carefully erase any remaining pencil marks.

Christmas star

Embroider all the elements from the main template using Sulky mixed thread 7027 and filling-in stitch before working in the beads. Sew each bead between two holes, as illustrated below. Once you have sewn a row of five beads, take the needle and thread from the reverse to the front and push it in a single pass through the whole row of beads and then back to the reverse. This thread will help to hold the beads in a beautifully straight line.

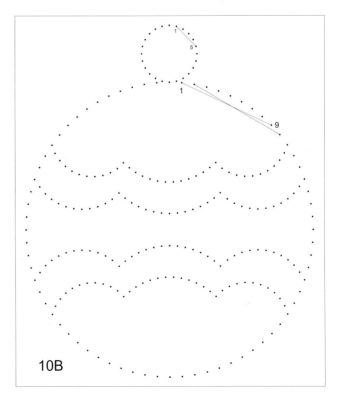

10B

Christmas bauble

Embroider the bauble using circle stitch 1–9 and the hanger using circle stitch 1–5. The thread is Sulky gold 7007. The beads used are about 2mm (⅛in) across.
Again sew the beads as in the drawing opposite. Once all the beads in a curve have been attached, run a thread through them. Pass the needle through a group of about four beads at a time and then through the next group.

Christmas tree

Use long stem stitch to embroider the branches of the tree. The stitch length is given on the pricking template. Sew on the beads as in the drawing opposite.

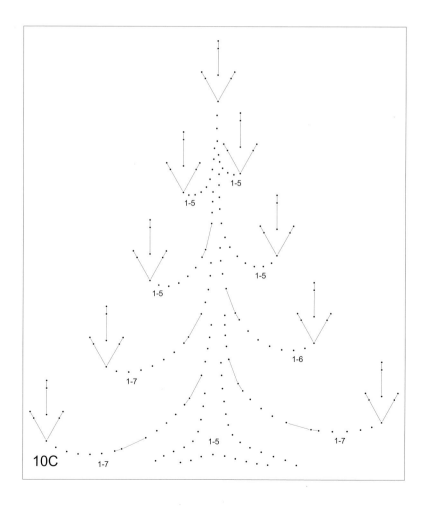

Y

Z